DATE DUE

Reindeer

Reindeer

Mary Ann McDonald

THE CHILD'S WORLD®, INC.

Library of Congress Cataloging-in-Publication Data
McDonald, Mary Ann.
Reindeer / by Mary Ann McDonald.
p.   cm.
Includes index.
Summary: Describes the physical characteristics,
behavior, habitat, and life cycle of reindeer.
ISBN 1-56766-491-1 (lib. bdg. : alk paper)
1. Reindeer—Juvenile literature.   [1. Reindeer.]   I. Title.
QL737.U55M27   1998
599.65'8—dc21   97-44647
CIP
AC

Photo Credits

ANIMALS ANIMALS © Fran Coleman: 20
ANIMALS ANIMALS © Robert Maier: 26
© 1994 Darrell Gulin/Dembinsky Photo Assoc. Inc: 23
© 1997 DPA/Dembinsky Photo Assoc. Inc: 16
© Joe McDonald: 2, 13
© 1992 Mike Barlow/Dembinsky Photo Assoc. Inc: 15
© 1993 Mike Barlow/Dembinsky Photo Assoc. Inc: 6, 30
© 1994 Mike Barlow/Dembinsky Photo Assoc. Inc: cover
© Natalie Fobes/Tony Stone Images: 24
© Paul Harris/Tony Stone Images: 29
© 1997 Russ Gutshall/Dembinsky Photo Assoc. Inc: 10
© 1997 Sharon Cummings/Dembinsky Photo Assoc. Inc: 9
© Tom McHugh, The National Audubon Society Collection/PR: 19

On the cover...

Front cover: This adult reindeer is walking on the Alaskan tundra.
Page 2: This hungry reindeer is eating some grass.

Table of Contents

In some parts of the world, the weather stays cool all year long. The ground is rocky and muddy, and short grasses grow everywhere. Places like this are called the *tundra*. Not many animals like to live on the tundra. But one creature spends much of its life here. What could it be? It's a reindeer!

What Are Reindeer?

Reindeer belong to the same group of animals as deer and elk. They are large and brown and have long legs. The long hair on their throats and bellies is a lighter color. They have very large, rounded hooves and short tails.

There are 23 different kinds of reindeer in the world. The best-known kind is called the *caribou*. It lives in Europe, Asia, and North America. Caribou like cold weather. In North America, caribou live wild in the Far North.

This caribou is looking for something to eat. ⇒

Male reindeer, called **bulls**, have long pieces of
bone that grow out of their heads. These are called
antlers. Female reindeer, called **cows**, have antlers,
too. Reindeer antlers are much different from those of
deer and elk. A reindeer's antler forms a flat, shovel-
like branch on one side that reaches down over the
reindeer's nose.

⇐ This reindeer bull has beautiful antlers.

Are Antlers and Horns Different?

Both horns and antlers grow from the top of an animal's head. But horns grow for the animal's entire life. Cows, bighorn sheep, and antelope all have horns. Horns keep growing and never fall off.

Animals that have antlers, on the other hand, lose their antlers once a year. When the old antlers fall off, newer, bigger antlers grow in their place. Moose, elk, deer, and reindeer all grow new antlers every year.

This older reindeer has very big antlers. ⇒

In early spring, the new antlers start growing out of two bony stumps. These new antlers are covered with a soft, furry skin called **velvet**. When the new antlers stop growing, the animal rubs off the velvet and polishes the antlers against trees and bushes.

This reindeer has rubbed off almost all of its new velvet. ⇒

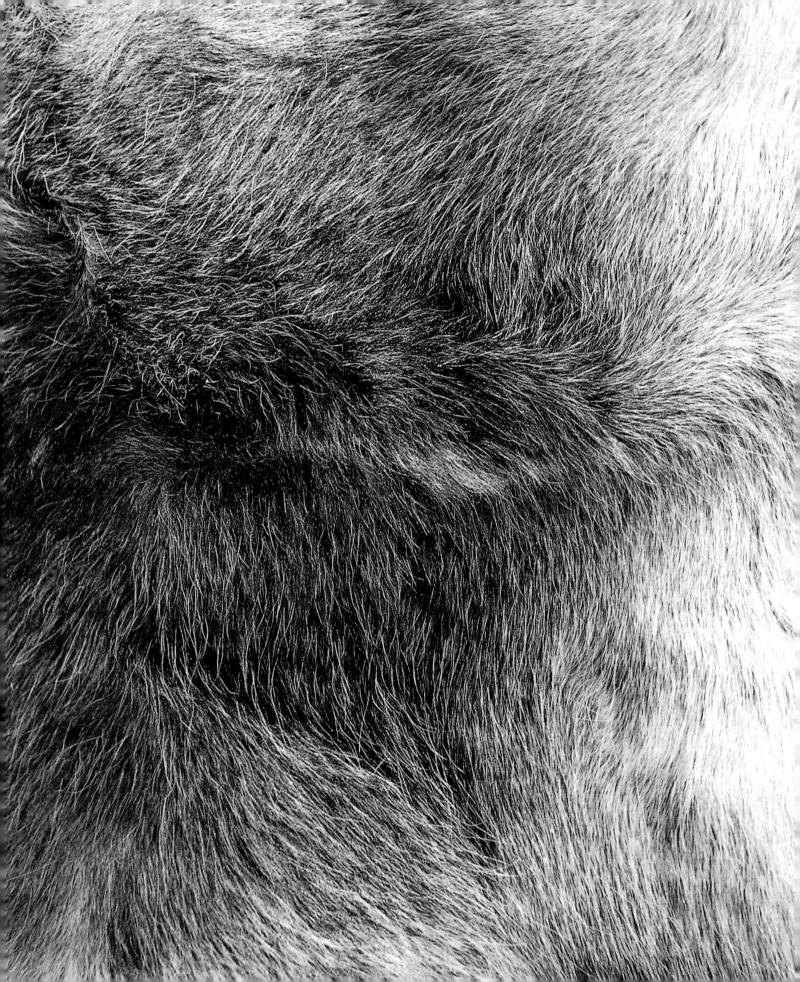

How Do Reindeer Survive in the Cold?

Many reindeer live in areas that are very cold for most of the year. To keep warm, the reindeer have two coats of fur. The outer fur is made up of long, tough hairs. These hairs are hollow to help trap warmth. Underneath the outer layer is a short undercoat of fine hairs. This inner layer is very soft and warm.

From close up, it is easy to see how thick this reindeer's fur is.

What Are Reindeer's Feet Like?

Reindeer's large, rounded feet are specially made for life in cold weather. Reindeer use their feet like shovels for digging through the snow. The wide, flat shape helps the reindeer run in the snow, too. The edges of the hooves are long, to keep the reindeer from slipping too much on the ice.

This reindeer is trying to scratch its nose with its back foot. ⇒

Reindeer feet make a funny clicking noise you can hear up to 90 feet away! At first people thought this noise came from the hooves clicking together as the reindeer walked. But it is really caused by muscles moving across the bones in the reindeers' feet. When reindeer gather together, the noise of thousands of clicking feet helps keep enemies away. It is also a comforting sound for the reindeer during the long, dark nights.

⇐ These reindeer are making clicking noises as they search for food.   21

What Do Reindeer Eat?

Reindeer eat only plants. During warmer weather, they eat several different types of grasses, leaves, and berries. Their main food, though, is a strange plant called *lichen* that grows on rocks and on the ground. During the summer, lichen is easy to find. But in the winter, reindeer must dig through the snow with their front hooves to find the frozen plants.

Reindeer often eat these *lichen* and *red bearberry* plants. ⇒

Every fall, North America's wild caribou travel hundreds of miles from their summer home to their winter home. In the spring, they move back again. This yearly movement from one area to another is called **migration**. The caribou migration is an incredible sight. Thousands of animals journey together to find food, warm weather, and safe places to have their babies.

A few months after mating, reindeer cows give birth to a single baby, or **calf**. Usually all the mothers have their babies within a few days of each other. The calves stay close to their mothers all summer. They learn how to eat plants and escape danger. When the weather turns cold again, they travel with the rest of the reindeer back to the thick forests for the winter.

⇐ This reindeer calf is eating some green grass.

Are Reindeer Important?

Reindeer have been important to people in northern areas for thousands of years. Reindeer have been raised and hunted for their meat and their skins. And some people have even been able to train reindeer to pull sleds!

This Russian herder is taking his reindeer to another area. ⇒

People have also caused harm to reindeer. In the Far North, drilling for oil has damaged some lands where caribou live. People have also disturbed the paths caribou need to follow on their migrations. We need to preserve places where the reindeer live. Then we can make sure that plenty of reindeer will still be around for people to see and learn about.

⟸ This caribou is watching other caribou on the Alaskan tundra.   31

Glossary

antlers (ANT–lerz)
Antlers are pieces of bone that grow out of a reindeer's head. The antlers are used for fighting and protection.

bulls (BULLZ)
Male reindeer are called bulls.

calf (KAFF)
A baby reindeer is called a calf. The mother usually gives birth to only one calf at a time.

cows (KOWZ)
Female reindeer are called cows. Unlike other female deer and elk, reindeer cows have antlers.

migration (my-GRAY-shun)
Migration is a yearly movement from one area to another. North American caribou migrate hundreds of miles from their summer home on the tundra to their forested winter feeding ground.

velvet (VELL-vet)
Velvet is a soft, furry skin that covers the newly grown antlers of a reindeer or deer. The velvet rubs off when the antlers are fully grown.

Index